Sam Illaiee

Healthcare
Interview Cheat Code

The Ebook

*Interview Intelligence:
Outthink,
Outperform,
Get Hired*

Tips through Hundreds of satisfied healthcare staff now in your hands!

THE HOW TO:
HEALTHCARE JOB INTERVIEW CHEAT CODE

BY SAM ILLAIEE

© Sam Illaiee 2024 All rights reserved

The characters and events portrayed in this book are fictitious. Any similarity to real persons, living or dead, is coincidental and not intended by the author.

No part of this book may be reproduced, or stored in a retrieval system, or transmitted in any form or by any means, electronic, mechanical, photocopying, recording, or otherwise, without express written permission of the publisher.

Cover design by: Sam Illaiee

Introduction	5
Crafting Your Personal Statement - The Art of Self-Presentation	10
Interview Questions - They will always be based around these	18
Interview Questions - The art of answering	24
Recognizing Red Flags and Reading the Room	43
Sealing the Deal and Graceful Exits	53
Final Thoughts	63
About the Author	69

INTRODUCTION

Are you tired of feeling nervous and unprepared when walking into job interviews? Do you find yourself stumbling over your words, unsure of how to effectively showcase your skills and experience? Perhaps you've left interviews feeling like you didn't quite hit the mark, unable to truly convey your value to potential employers. . Our 'how to interveiw for NHS jobs is a more comprehensive guide; with even more proven success . Get it here https://amzn.to/4clO3ax

My Name is Sam Illaiee. having worked in. healthcare for much of my career (having initially trained as a Pharmacist) i have many experiences through job applications and have coach a fair few people to success when it come to getting the next role.

In today's competitive job market, nailing the interview is more crucial than ever. But what separates a good interview from a great one? How can you ensure that you stand out from the crowd and leave a lasting impression?

This book is designed to answer these pressing questions and many more:

1. How do you craft a compelling personal narrative that resonates with interviewers?

2. What's the secret to discussing your weaknesses without undermining your candidacy?

3. How can you demonstrate your value to a company you're eager to join?

4. What strategies can you employ to handle high-pressure situations with grace?

5. How do you address challenges from your past work experiences positively?

6. What's the best way to manage multiple responsibilities and priorities?

7. How can you turn difficult workplace situations into examples of your problem-solving skills?

Whether you're a recent graduate entering the job market for the first time, a seasoned professional looking to make a career change, or someone who simply wants to sharpen their interview skills, this guide has something for you.

In the following chapters, we'll break down each aspect of the interview process, providing you with practical strategies, real-world examples, and expert insights. You'll learn how to prepare thoroughly, respond confidently, and follow up effectively.

By the time you finish this book, you'll have the tools and confidence to transform your interview performance. You'll be ready to articulate your value, connect with interviewers, and ultimately land the job you've been dreaming of.

Let's begin your journey to interview success."

1. CRAFTING YOUR PERSONAL STATEMENT - THE ART OF SELF-PRESENTATION

Before you interview, your personal statement is often your first opportunity to make a lasting impression on potential employers. It's not just about listing your qualifications; it's about telling your professional story in a compelling way that answers three crucial questions: Why you? Why this role? Why this organization?

THE TRIAD OF PERSUASION: YOU, THE ROLE, AND THE ORGANIZATION

Why You?

This is your chance to showcase what makes you unique. Highlight your key skills, experiences, and achievements that are most relevant to the position. Don't just list them; demonstrate how they've shaped you into the ideal candidate. Example: "My five years of experience as a team lead, coupled with my innovative approach to client engagement strategies, have consistently resulted in a 30% annual increase in good outcomes."

Why This Role?

Explain how this specific position aligns with your career goals and how your skills make you a perfect fit. Show that you understand the role's requirements and how you can meet them.

Example: "The director position at your organisation offers the perfect opportunity for me to leverage my expertise in both acute and primary care integrating them, while taking on the leadership responsibilities I've been preparing for."

Why This Organization?

Demonstrate that you've done your research. Discuss the company's values, recent projects, or industry position that resonate with you. Show how your goals align with the organization's mission.

Example: "Your company's commitment to sustainable and innovative practices in the health industry aligns perfectly with my personal values and professional experience in modern healthcare initiatives."

The Importance of Evidencing Skills vs. Job Description

When addressing the job description, don't fall into the trap of simply repeating the requirements. Instead, provide concrete evidence of how you've demonstrated these skills in past roles.
Poor example: "I am a good communicator and team player."
Strong example: "In my role as Project Coordinator, I successfully led cross-functional teams of up to 15 members, facilitating clear communication that resulted in all projects being delivered on time and

within budget over a two-year period."

Use the STAR method (Situation, Task, Action, Result) to structure your examples. This approach provides a clear, concise way to demonstrate your skills in action.

The Critical Role of Grammar and Professionalism

Your personal statement is a reflection of your attention to detail and professionalism. Grammatical errors or sloppy writing can undermine even the most impressive qualifications.

Key tips for polishing your statement:

- Use active voice to make your writing more dynamic and engaging.
- Vary your sentence structure to maintain the reader's interest.
- Be concise — aim for clear, impactful statements rather than flowery language.
- Proofread multiple times, and consider having someone else review your statement.
- Use industry-specific terminology appropriately to demonstrate your knowledge.

Example of improvement:

Weak: "I helped the company make more money."

Strong: "I implemented a new customer retention strategy that increased annual revenue by 15%."

Tailoring Your Statement

Remember, your personal statement should be tailored for each application. Use the job description as a guide, but don't simply parrot it back. Instead, use it as a framework to highlight your most relevant experiences and skills.

Your personal statement is your chance to stand out from the crowd. By clearly articulating why you're the right person for the role and the organization, providing evidence of your skills, and presenting your case in a grammatically correct and professional manner, you set the stage for a successful application. Take the time to craft a compelling narrative that not only showcases your qualifications but also gives the reader a sense of who you are as a professional. This is your opportunity to make a powerful first impression — make it count.

YOUR PERSONAL STATEMENT IS A REFLECTION OF YOUR ATTENTION TO DETAIL AND PROFESSIONALISM

2.
INTERVIEW QUESTIONS - THEY WILL ALWAYS BE BASED AROUND THESE

Welcome to our Lead the Way Job Interview Cheat Sheet and you can find the podcast from the link below https://podcasters.spotify.com/pod/show/camhssteps

It's a very special release because of the number of people who have benefitted from my coaching using these tools Let's break down the key questions you might face and then how to approach them professionally:

Ice Breakers

Introducing yourself: Share your career journey concisely, highlighting experiences relevant to the role. Mention a few personal interests to round out your profile.

Explaining your interest in the company: Demonstrate your research on the company. Discuss how your skills align with their needs and how the role fits your career goals.

Differentiating yourself: Highlight your top strengths with specific examples. Mention any unique skills or experiences that set you apart.

Challenge!

Addressing missed deadlines: Describe a situation where you faced a deadline challenge. Explain how you communicated the issue and what you learned from the experience.

Discussing your weaknesses: Be honest about areas for improvement. Focus on skills you're actively developing and how you're addressing them.

Handling pressure: Share a specific example of working under pressure. Describe your strategies for managing stress and maintaining productivity.

Working with difficult colleagues: Explain a situation where you successfully collaborated with a challenging team member. Emphasize your communication and problem-solving skills.

Strategy!

Reasons for leaving your current job: Frame your answer positively, focusing on seeking new opportunities for growth rather than criticizing your current employer.

Managing multiple responsibilities: Describe how you organize and prioritize tasks. Provide an example of successfully juggling various duties.

Your toughest challenge: Use the STAR method (Situation, Task, Action, Result) to describe a complex problem you solved. Choose an example that showcases your skills relevant to the job.

Questions for the interviewer: Always have thoughtful questions prepared. This shows your genuine interest in the role and company.

Remember, keep your responses concise yet informative. Aim for about two minutes per answer, and always relate your experiences back to the job at hand.
In our next segment, we'll dive deeper into each of these points and provide specific examples to help you craft compelling responses."

USE THE STAR METHOD (SITUATION, TASK, ACTION, RESULT) TO DESCRIBE A COMPLEX PROBLEM YOU SOLVED. CHOOSE AN EXAMPLE THAT SHOWCASES YOUR SKILLS RELEVANT TO THE JOB

3.
INTERVIEW QUESTIONS - THE ART OF ANSWERING

We're diving into the art of acing job interviews. I'll break down the essential questions you'll face and give you examples of what not to say, followed by winning responses. Let's get started.

Tell me about yourself and your background

Poor response: "Well, um, I graduated college a few years ago and I've been working at Company X since then. I like watching Netflix and hanging out with friends on weekends."

Good response: "I've spent the last five years honing my skills in x healthcare speciality, specializing in (field A clinical) and Field b- non clinical . My journey began at a (lowest grade) where I wore many hats, giving me a holistic view of the industry. Outside of work, I'm an avid rock climber, which has taught me a lot about perseverance and strategic thinking - skills I bring to my professional life as well."

Why do you want to work for this company?

Poor response: "I saw you were hiring and the salary looked good.

Plus, your office is close to my apartment."

Good response: "I've been following your company's innovative approach to patient care for years. Your recent projects on (what you have read in news) aligns perfectly with my passion for(whatever evidence base) . I believe my experience in leadership and developing services and leaders development could contribute significantly to your mission of creating outstanding solutions."

What sets you apart from other applicants?

Poor response: "I'm a hard worker and a quick learner. I'm also really good with people."

Good response: "My unique blend of clinical expertise and operational/strategic problem-solving sets me apart. For instance, in my previous role, I developed a custom analytics tool that increased our team's efficiency by 30%. This demonstrates not only my leadership skills but also my ability to identify and solve complex business challenges working across departments collaboratively."

Tell me about a time when you couldn't meet a deadline. How did you handle it?

Poor response: "I once missed a big deadline and my boss was really mad. It was pretty stressful."

Good response: "In my last project, we faced an unexpected technical issue that threatened our launch date. I immediately communicated the situation to stakeholders and proposed a solution. We reprioritized tasks, I put in extra hours, and delegated effectively. While we missed the original deadline by two days, our transparent communication and quick problem-solving actually strengthened client trust."

What is the hardest problem you've ever tackled?

Poor response: "Probably my exam final in college. That was really tough."

Good response: "The most challenging problem I faced was

optimizing our company's supply chain during the global pandemic. Using the STAR method: The Situation was a 40% drop in our usual ' capacity. My Task was to maintain service levels despite this setback. My Action involved rapidly vetting new staff, negotiating contracts, and implementing a real-time inventory tracking system. The Result was a 95% maintenance of our clinical capacity and a new, more resilient operational model that we still use today as we meet surge during ebb and flow."

Remember, the key to interview success is preparation, authenticity, and the ability to articulate your value clearly. In our next segment, we'll dive deeper into handling tough questions about weaknesses and career transitions.

Take a few minutes to reflect.....

.... We're continuing our deep dive into mastering job interviews. Let's explore more crucial questions and how to tackle them effectively.

What are your weaknesses and how would you improve them?

Poor response: "I don't really have any weaknesses. I'm pretty much good at everything I do."

Good response: "One area I'm actively working on is public speaking. While I'm confident in small group settings, I've realized the importance of being able to present to larger audiences in my field. To address this, I've joined a local Toastmasters club and have been volunteering to lead more team presentations. I've already seen improvement in my confidence and delivery, but I'm committed to ongoing growth in this area."

How do you deal with pressure or stressful situations?

Poor response: "I don't really get stressed. I just kind of go with the flow and things usually work out."

Good response: "I've developed several strategies for managing pressure over the years. For example, when facing a tight deadline on a complex project, I break the work into smaller, manageable tasks and prioritize them. I also practice mindfulness techniques like deep breathing to stay focused. In my previous role, these methods helped me successfully lead a team through a high-stakes new service launch under significant time constraints. We not only met our deadline but exceeded our quality targets."

Share an example of how you handled working with someone who's difficult.

Poor response: "I once had a really annoying coworker. I just tried to avoid them as much as possible."

Good response: "In my last role, I collaborated with a colleague who i initially felt was difficult. They had a very different communication style and work approach. Initially, this led to some misunderstandings and tension. I took the initiative to schedule a one-on-one meeting where we openly discussed our working styles and expectations. By actively listening and showing empathy, we found common ground. We agreed on a communication protocol that worked for both of us, which not only resolved our issues but actually led to a highly productive partnership on subsequent projects."

Why do you want to leave your current place of work?

Poor response: "My boss is terrible, and the company culture is toxic. I can't wait to get out of there."

Good response: "While I've gained valuable experience in my current role and appreciate the opportunities I've had, I'm looking for new challenges that align more closely with my long-term career goals. Specifically, I'm eager to take on more leadership responsibilities and work on larger-scale projects. From what I've learned about this position, it seems to offer the growth and development opportunities I'm seeking at this stage in my career."

Describe a situation where you had to handle multiple responsibilities.

Poor response: "I'm always juggling a lot of stuff. It's pretty overwhelming, but I manage somehow."

Good response: "In my role as a project manager, I often handle multiple high-priority tasks simultaneously. For instance, last quarter I was overseeing the launch of our new software product while also managing the onboarding of two new team members and preparing for a crucial client presentation. To ensure everything was accomplished effectively, I implemented a detailed project management system using Asana, delegated tasks where appropriate, and block-scheduled my time for different responsibilities. This approach allowed me to successfully launch the product on time, fully integrate the new team members, and deliver a compelling presentation that secured a major client contract."

Do you have any questions for us?

Poor response: "No, I think you've covered everything."

Good response: "Yes, I have a few questions. First, could you tell me more about the team I'd be working with and the current projects they're focused on? Second, what do you see as the biggest challenges and opportunities for this role in the next year? Lastly, how does the company support professional development and growth for its employees?"

Remember, the key to nailing these questions is not just having polished answers, but delivering them with authenticity and enthusiasm. Your responses should reflect your genuine experiences and align with the company's values and needs.

In our next segment, we'll discuss how to follow up after the interview and negotiate your offer. Until then, keep refining your stories and practicing your responses. The more prepared you are, the more confident you'll feel walking into that interview room."

"Now to our final segment on mastering job interviews. We've covered a lot of ground, but before we wrap up, let's discuss some overarching strategies that will elevate your interview performance.

The power of storytelling

Poor approach: Giving vague, general answers without concrete examples.

Good approach: "Throughout your interview, weave in compelling stories that showcase your skills and experiences. Remember the STAR method - Situation, Task, Action, Result. For instance, don't just say you're good at problem-solving. Instead, share a specific story about a time you overcame a significant challenge, the actions you took, and the positive outcome you achieved. This approach not only makes your answers more engaging but also more memorable to the interviewer.

Body language and non-verbal communication

Poor approach: Slouching, avoiding eye contact, or fidgeting nervously.

Good approach: "Your non-verbal cues speak volumes. Maintain good posture, make appropriate eye contact, and offer a firm handshake. Practice active listening by nodding and engaging with the interviewer's questions. These subtle cues demonstrate confidence, interest, and professionalism.

Research and preparation

Poor approach: Having only surface-level knowledge about the company and role.

Good approach: "Deep research is your secret weapon. Go beyond the company's website. Read recent news articles, understand their market position, and familiarize yourself with their products or services. Use this knowledge to ask insightful questions and draw connections between your experience and the company's needs.

Follow-up and post-interview etiquette

Poor approach: Failing to follow up or sending a generic thank-you email.

Good approach: "Within 24 hours of your interview, send a personalized thank-you email to each interviewer. Reference specific points from your conversation to show you were engaged and attentive. This is also an opportunity to briefly reiterate your interest in the role and how you can add value to their team.

Remember, a job interview is not just about showcasing your skills — it's about demonstrating how you can solve problems for the company.

EVERY ANSWER YOU GIVE SHOULD, IN SOME WAY, ILLUSTRATE THE VALUE YOU'LL BRING TO THE ROLE AND THE ORGANIZATION.

4.
RECOGNIZING RED FLAGS AND READING THE ROOM

While you're focused on presenting your best self during an interview, it's equally important to be attuned to the signals the interviewer and company are sending. This chapter will help you identify potential warning signs, recognize when you need to adjust your approach, and determine if the opportunity is genuinely right for you.

TOXIC VIBES: WHEN THE CULTURE RAISES CONCERNS

Dismissive or Disrespectful Behaviour

- Red Flag: Interviewers who interrupt, talk over you, or display condescending attitudes.
- What it Might Mean: Poor communication culture or lack of respect for employees.

Excessive Negativity About Previous Employees

- Red Flag: Unprompted criticism of former team members or excessive company turnover.
- What it Might Mean: Potential management issues or a blame-oriented culture.

Inconsistent Information

- Red Flag: Different interviewers provide conflicting details about the role or company.
- What it Might Mean: Poor internal communication or disorganization.

Pressure to Accept Immediately

- Red Flag: Rushing you to make a decision without proper consideration.
- What it Might Mean: Desperation to fill the role or manipulative hiring practices.

SIGNS THE INTERVIEW ISN'T GOING WELL AND HOW TO PIVOT

Short, Disengaged Responses

Sign: The interviewer gives brief answers and doesn't elaborate.
How to Pivot: Ask more engaging questions about the company's challenges or future projects.

Lack of Follow-up Questions

Sign: The interviewer doesn't probe deeper into your responses.
How to Pivot: Offer additional relevant information or ask if they'd like you to expand on any points.

Body Language Cues

Sign: Crossed arms, lack of eye contact, or frequently checking the time.
How to Pivot: Adjust your energy, be more concise, or directly ask if you're addressing their key concerns.

Abrupt Ending

Sign: The interview ends much earlier than scheduled without explanation.
How to Pivot: If possible, ask for feedback or if there's anything else you can clarify about your qualifications.

INDICATORS OF GENUINE INTEREST

Engaged Discussion

Positive Sign: The conversation flows naturally, with back-and-forth dialogue.
What it Means: You've captured their interest and are seen as a viable candidate.

Introduction to Team Members

Positive Sign: You're introduced to potential colleagues or given an office tour.
What it Means: They're seriously considering you for the role.

Detailed Discussion of Next Steps

Positive Sign: Clear information about the hiring timeline and future rounds.
What it Means: You're likely moving forward in the process.

Questions About Your Availability and Notice Period

Positive Sign: Inquiries about when you could potentially start.
What it Means: They're envisioning you in the role.

WHEN THEY'RE NOT REALLY INTERESTED

Vague Responses About the Role or Company Future

Sign: Inability or unwillingness to provide specifics about the position or company plans.
What it Might Mean: The role may not be well-defined or there might be underlying issues.

Focus on Overqualification

Sign: Repeated comments about your experience exceeding the role's requirements.
What it Might Mean: Concerns about your fit or longevity in the position.

Lack of Selling the Opportunity

Sign: No attempt to highlight the benefits of working for the company. What it Might Mean: They may have other candidates in mind or internal hiring preferences.

Redirection to Other Roles

Sign: Suggestions that you might be better suited for a different position. What it Might Mean: They don't see you as a fit for this specific role but value your overall profile.

Being aware of these signals during the interview process is crucial for making informed decisions about your career. Remember, an interview is a two-way street. While you're being evaluated, you should also be assessing whether the company and role are the right fit for you.

If you notice red flags, trust your instincts but also consider seeking clarification. Sometimes, what seems like a warning sign might be a misunderstanding that can be resolved through open communication.

On the other hand, if you sense the interview isn't going well, stay positive and try to turn things around using the pivot strategies mentioned. Even if this particular opportunity doesn't work out, maintaining professionalism can leave a good impression for future possibilities.

Ultimately, the goal is to find a role and company where you can thrive.

By being attentive to these signals, you're better equipped to make decisions that align with your career goals and values.

"IF YOU SENSE THE INTERVIEW ISN'T GOING WELL, STAY POSITIVE AND TRY TO TURN THINGS AROUND USING THE PIVOT STRATEGIES"

5.
SEALING THE DEAL AND GRACEFUL EXITS

Congratulations on your successful interview! Now, it's time to navigate the delicate processes of negotiation and leaving your current role. This chapter will guide you through securing the best possible terms for your new position and departing from your current job on a positive note.

PART 1: NEGOTIATING BETTER CONDITIONS

Do Your Research

Understand industry standards for salary and benefits for your role and location.
Use resources like Glassdoor, PayScale, and professional associations for data.

Know Your Worth

Quantify your achievements and their impact on previous employers. Be prepared to articulate why you deserve what you're asking for.

Consider the Entire Package

Look beyond salary — consider benefits, work-life balance, professional development opportunities, and other perks.

Prioritize what's most important to you.

Start High, But Be Realistic

Begin negotiations at the upper end of your researched range.
Be prepared to justify your ask with concrete examples of your value.

Use Positive Language

Frame requests in terms of mutual benefit: "I'm excited about contributing to the team. To fully commit my energy to this role, I'm hoping we can discuss..."

Be Prepared to Compromise

Have a "walk away" number in mind, but also be open to creative solutions.
Consider non-monetary benefits if there's limited flexibility on salary.

Get It in Writing

Once you've reached an agreement, ensure all details are included in your offer letter.

PART 2: EXITING YOUR CURRENT ROLE WITH GRACE

Timing Is Everything

Wait until you have a signed offer letter before giving notice.

Provide standard notice (usually two weeks) unless your contract specifies otherwise.

Inform Your Manager First

Schedule a face-to-face meeting (or video call) with your direct supervisor.
Be prepared for various reactions and questions about your decision.

Be Positive and Grateful

Express appreciation for the opportunities and experiences you've had.
Focus on how the role has contributed to your professional growth.

Offer to Assist with the Transition

Propose a plan to hand over your responsibilities.
Offer to train your replacement if time allows.

Maintain Professionalism Until the End

Continue to perform at your best during your notice period.
Avoid negative comments about the company or colleagues.

Prepare a Thorough Handover

Document your processes and ongoing projects.
Update your team on the status of your work.

Say Proper Goodbyes

Personally thank colleagues who have been particularly supportive. Consider writing thank-you notes to mentors or key team members.

Conduct an Exit Interview Positively

If asked to participate in an exit interview, provide constructive feedback.
Focus on improvement suggestions rather than complaints.

Leave the Door Open

Network with colleagues you'd like to stay in touch with.
Connect on LinkedIn if you haven't already.

Reflect on Lessons Learned

Consider what you've gained from this role and how it will benefit you moving forward.

Example Script for Resignation:

"*Thank you for meeting with me. I wanted to let you know that I've accepted a new position at another company. My last day here will be [date]. I'm grateful for the opportunities I've had to grow and contribute here. I'd like to ensure a smooth transition, so I've prepared a handover plan for my current projects. Please let me know how I can best support the team during this transition period.*"

Negotiating better conditions and exiting your current role professionally are crucial steps in your career journey. By approaching negotiations with confidence and research, you set yourself up for success in your new role. Similarly, leaving your current job with grace and gratitude ensures you maintain positive relationships and a strong professional reputation.

Remember, the business world is often smaller than it seems. The colleagues you leave behind today may become valuable connections or even future employers. By handling your exit thoughtfully, you're not just closing a chapter – you're opening doors for future opportunities.

Your departure should leave your current employer feeling that they're losing a valuable team member, but also respecting your decision to grow professionally. This approach ensures you'll be remembered fondly and potentially welcomed back if paths cross again in the future.

"NETWORK WITH COLLEAGUES YOU'D LIKE TO STAY IN TOUCH WITH. CONNECT ON LINKEDIN IF YOU HAVEN'T ALREADY"

6.
FINAL THOUGHTS

As an experienced NHS senior manager who has guided over 100 individuals to successful job placements, I've witnessed firsthand the transformative power of effective interview skills. This book distills decades of insights and practical strategies that have consistently helped candidates secure their desired roles.

The interview process is far more than a simple question-and-answer session. It's a unique opportunity to showcase your organizational prowess, interpersonal skills, and professional acumen. The true art lies in effectively communicating your value proposition within the constraints of a 30-60 minute interaction.

Remember, every question is an opening to demonstrate your capabilities. When discussing your experiences, don't just recite facts—illustrate how you've navigated challenges, collaborated with diverse teams, and driven meaningful outcomes. These narratives paint a vivid picture of your potential contributions to the prospective employer.

Preparation is key, but authenticity is equally crucial. The most compelling candidates are those who balance thorough research with genuine enthusiasm for the role and organization. Let your passion for your field shine through, tempered with professional poise.

While this book provides a comprehensive framework for interview success, each career journey is unique. For those seeking personalized guidance to navigate their specific challenges and aspirations, I offer one-on-one coaching services. Whether you're looking to refine your interview technique, develop a compelling personal brand, or strategize your career progression, tailored support can be invaluable.

My sincere hope is that the strategies and insights shared in these pages empower you to approach your next interview with confidence and clarity. Remember, an interview is not just about securing a job—it's about finding the right fit for your skills, values, and career goals.

As you embark on your next professional chapter, carry with you the knowledge that with proper preparation and the right mindset, you have the power to turn each interview into an opportunity for growth and success.

For those interested in taking their interview skills to the next level or seeking personalized career guidance, I invite you to explore my coaching services. Together, we can work on honing your unique professional narrative and developing strategies tailored to your career aspirations.

Sam ILLAIEE NHS Senior Manager & Career Coach

Email and book me: camhssteps@gmail.com

podcast : https://podcasters.spotify.com/pod/show/camhssteps

"THANK YOU FOR ENTRUSTING ME TO BE A PART OF YOUR PROFESSIONAL JOURNEY. I WISH YOU THE VERY BEST IN YOUR CAREER ENDEAVORS AND LOOK FORWARD TO THE POSSIBILITY OF WORKING TOGETHER TO ACHIEVE YOUR GOALS"

ABOUT THE AUTHOR

Sam Illaiee, also known as Abdool Samad Illaiee, is a multifaceted professional with a diverse background. He is a pharmacist, NHS Senior Manager, and Functional Medicine practitioner with a deep commitment to healthcare and community well-being.

A devout Muslim, Sam is also an entrepreneur, chef, and family man, balancing his professional pursuits with his personal life. He is passionate about writing and sharing knowledge on various topics, including mental health, cognitive biases, and Islamic teachings. Sam is the founder of CAMHSSTEPS.COM Limited, where he serves as Director, and he is actively involved in the healthcare and digital education sectors.

Sam is also a content creator, leveraging platforms like YouTube and TikTok to discuss topics related to mental health, leadership, and Islamic principles.

His work aims to bridge gaps between communities and promote understanding through education and dialogue.

Sam has honed his skills in organizational management, strategic planning, and talent development.

As a passionate advocate for professional growth, Sam has dedicated a significant portion of his career to mentoring and coaching. He has successfully guided over 100 individuals through the intricacies of job searching, interview preparation, and career advancement within the healthcare sector and beyond.

Sam's expertise lies in his ability to distill complex interview processes into actionable strategies. His approach combines deep industry knowledge with a keen understanding of human dynamics, enabling candidates to showcase their best selves during crucial career moments.

In addition to his work with the NHS, Sam is a sought-after career coach, offering personalized guidance to professionals at various stages of their careers. His coaching philosophy emphasizes authenticity, strategic preparation, and the art of effective communication.

Through this book and his coaching services, Sam aims to share his insights and proven techniques with a wider audience, empowering job seekers to navigate the interview process with confidence and success.

For more information about Sam's coaching services or to connect with him, please contact me through email address or socials

NOTES

NOTES

NOTES

NOTES

NOTES

NOTES

NOTES

NOTES

www.ingramcontent.com/pod-product-compliance
Lightning Source LLC
Chambersburg PA
CBHW070354230526
45471CB00006B/2567